WHAT'S INSIDE?
BATTLESHIPS AND AIRCRAFT CARRIERS

WHAT'S INSIDE?
BATTLESHIPS AND AIRCRAFT CARRIERS

Sandy Creek
NEW YORK

Sandy Creek
NEW YORK

An Imprint of Sterling Publishing
387 Park Avenue South
New York, NY 10016

Editorial and design by
Amber Books Ltd
74–77 White Lion Street
London N1 9PF
United Kingdom

Series Editor: Michael Spilling
Project Editor: Sarah Uttridge
Design: Brian Rust and Andrew Easton
Picture Research: Terry Forshaw

ISBN 978-1-4351-5367-7

Manufactured in China
Lot #:
2 4 6 8 10 9 7 5 3 1
09/12

Picture Credits
Photographs
Art-Tech/Aerospace: 10, 11, 15, 16, 20, 26, 27
Art-Tech/MARS: 22; Cody Images: 6, 12, 14, 18, 19, 23, 24, 32
Corbis: 8; Library of Congress: 7; Public Domain: 28
U.S. Department of Defense: 3, 42, 43, 44
U.S. Navy: 30, 31, 34, 35, 36, 38, 39, 40
Artworks
Art-Tech/Aerospace: 1, 37, 41, 45
Art-Tech/De Agostini: 9, 13, 17, 21, 25, 29, 33

Contents

HMS Dreadnought (1906)

The first modern battleship was the British HMS *Dreadnought*. The warship joined the Royal Navy in 1906 and was the fastest, best-armed ship in the fleet.

Soon after *Dreadnought* was **launched**, other countries began improving their navies and building their own battleships. This race to construct faster, more powerful ships involved many of the countries that would soon fight against one another in World War I (1914–1918).

New Technologies

Dreadnought was built in the Portsmouth naval dockyard in England. It only took one year to build the battleship.

The gun turrets on the battleship *Dreadnought* had the ability to rotate. This allowed the ship's guns to aim at targets in different directions.

ship to go faster than other naval vessels of the time. HMS *Dreadnought* was able to reach speeds of up to 21 **knots**—or 24 miles per hour (39 km/h).

Big Guns

Battleships were built for their **firepower**. They could cause a great deal of damage to other ships and enemy targets on land. HMS *Dreadnought* was armed with ten 12-inch (305 mm) guns that were mounted on **turrets**. Each turret had two guns. The ten main guns of *Dreadnought* were able to hit targets as far away as 14 miles (22.5 km).

Dreadnought **did not participate in any of the major naval battles of World War I, but her powerful presence motivated other nations to begin building their own armored fleets.**

Unlike earlier ships that were **propelled** by sail or steam engines, HMS *Dreadnought* was the first large warship to use **turbine** engines. This new technology allowed the

Did you know?

• HMS *Dreadnought* started an arms **race** with other world powers, including Germany, France, Japan, and the United States.

• **HMS stands for "Her (or His) Majesty's ship."**

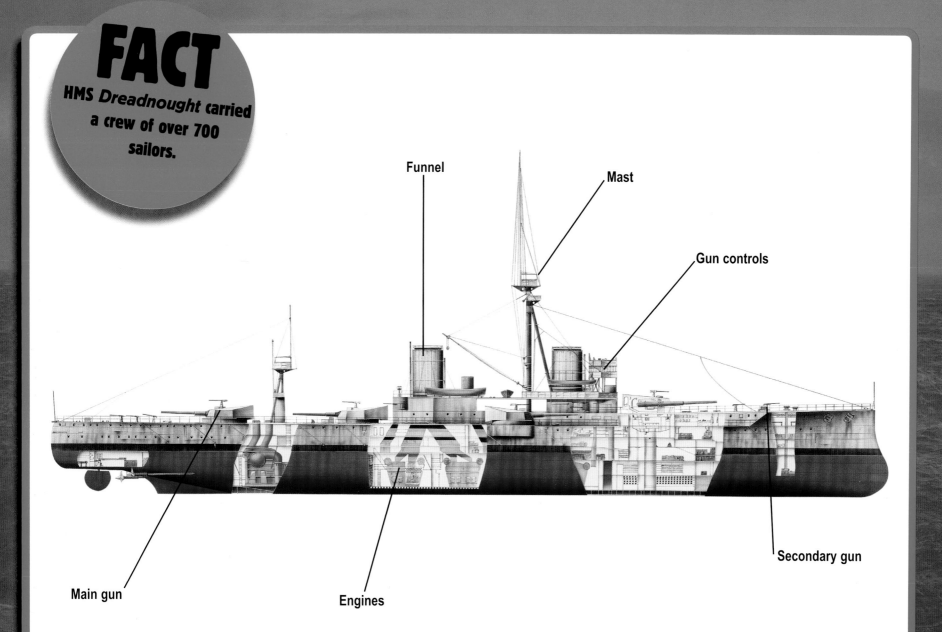

Funnel

Mast

Gun controls

Secondary gun

Main gun

Engines

HMS Hood (1918)

Known for being the largest naval ship built in the first half of 20th century, the British HMS *Hood* was launched on August 22, 1918. She served the Royal Navy for 23 years and was destroyed in 1941 by the German battleship *Bismarck*.

● ● ● ● ● ● ● ● ● ● ● ● ●

HMS *Hood* was named in honor of the Hood family, which included famous leaders who had served in the Royal Navy. Between World Wars I and II, *Hood* spent most of her time traveling around the world, displaying the power of the British Royal Navy.

Battle Cruiser

HMS *Hood* was classified as a **battle cruiser**. She was built with dynamic new engines that provided additional

HMS *Hood* was completed after World War I and did not enter battle until World War II.

Although lightly armored, *Hood* was able to deliver a powerful punch with her eight 15-inch (380 mm) guns.

horsepower. *Hood* was also built with less armor compared to other battleships of the time. The added horsepower and lighter armor allowed the warship to be faster than most other large ships.

Did you know?

• Adding the word "the" to a ship's name is incorrect. Instead of saying, "The *Bismarck* sank the *Hood*," it should be: "*Bismarck* sank *Hood*."

• Measuring 860 feet (262 m) long and 104 feet (37 m) wide, *Hood* did not have an equal in size until after World War II.

The Sinking of *Hood*

Although the battle cruiser *Hood* was built to outrun enemy warships, she was not designed to take heavy fire. Her thinly protected decks and sides were no match for the German battleship *Bismarck*. On May 24, 1941, these ships faced off in the North Atlantic. *Bismarck's* shells were able to break through *Hood*'s armor and the ship sank in minutes. Out of a crew of 1,400 men only three survived.

FACT

HMS *Hood* was able to reach speeds of 31 knots—close to 36 miles per hour (58 km/h).

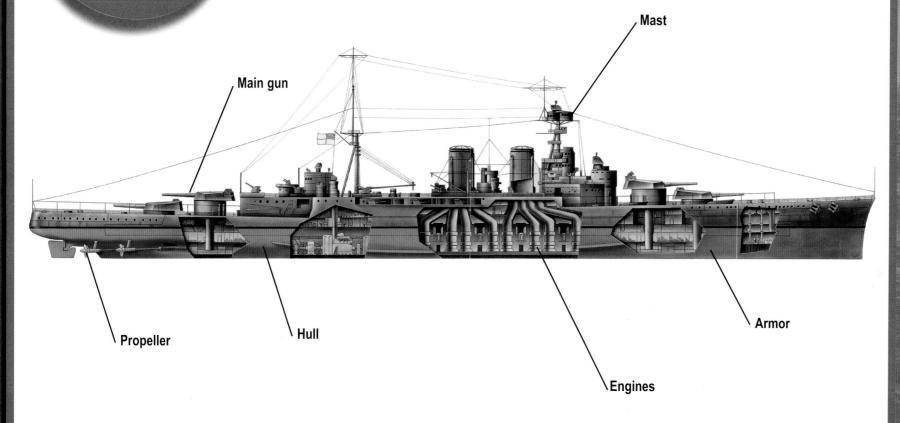

Main gun

Mast

Propeller

Hull

Engines

Armor

KMS Scharnhorst (1936)

The German-built Kriegsmarine (KMS) battleship *Scharnhorst* was launched in 1936 during Germany's period of rearmament before World War II (1939–1945). Most of her brief time of service was spent in the North Atlantic.

Together with a "sister" battleship, *Gneisenau*, *Scharnhorst* caused a great deal of damage to British shipping. Numerous British military and **merchant ships** were damaged or destroyed by *Scharnhorst*'s three powerful triple-gun turrets.

Operation Cerberus

After spending months trapped in the port of Brest, France, *Scharnhorst*, along with two other German

Captain Otto Ciliax inspects his men on the deck of the battleship *Scharnhorst*.

warships, set course for Germany. The journey back home, however, would not be an easy one. The German warships made what was known as "the

An Arado AR-196 sea plane is hoisted onto *Scharnhorst*'s deck.

Channel Dash," racing up the English Channel and avoiding **radar** detection and the threat of attack from nearby British naval bases.

Christmas 1942

After many close calls, *Scharnhorst* met her end on Christmas Day in 1942. Within a few hours of taking heavy fire from the British battleship *Duke of York*, the damaged *Scharnhorst* was torpedoed by two British cruisers. Out of a crew of 1,960, only 36 survived.

FACT

Scharnhorst carried three military sea planes used mainly to search for enemy ships.

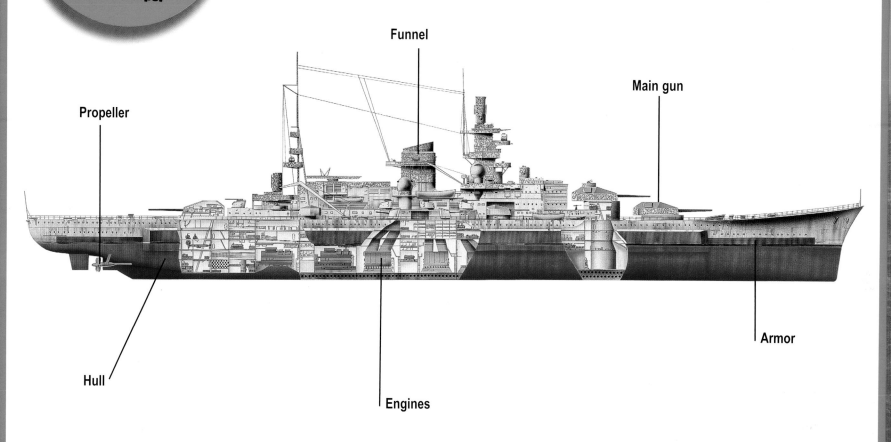

Funnel

Main gun

Propeller

Hull

Engines

Armor

USS Enterprise (1936)

The *Yorktown*-class aircraft carrier USS *Enterprise* was built in 1936 and commissioned on May 12, 1938. Away on a mission during the Japanese bombing of Pearl Harbor, *Enterprise* went on to fight in key battles in the Pacific.

Enterprise is the most decorated ship in U.S. history. It is also one of the few U.S. aircraft carriers to survive World War II.

Floating Airfields

These giant ships serve as moveable, floating airfields. They carry warplanes that support naval missions. USS *Enterprise* held 90 airplanes on her long, wide deck. These planes included fighter planes, **dive bombers**, and torpedo bombers, which were used

Enterprise played an important role in the Doolittle Raid on Tokyo, supporting the B-25 bombers that attacked Japan.

The Pacific Theater

Unlike other major warships in the U.S. Navy, *Enterprise* was not in port in Pearl Harbor, Hawaii, on December 7, 1941. As a result, she was spared from the Japanese surprise attack that brought the United States into World War II. In the months and years to follow, *Enterprise* would play a major role in key battles, including the Battle of the Philippine Sea, Guadalcanal, and the Battle of Leyte Gulf.

One of *Enterprise*'s main jobs was to protect other ships in the fleet from enemy aircraft. She also helped patrol the seas and look out for enemy ships and submarines.

against enemy ships. Planes were kept on the ship's deck as well as in special **hangars** below deck.

Did you know?

• USS *Enterprise* was also referred to as the "Lucky E," "Big E," and "Gray Ghost."

• Although the World War II–era USS *Enterprise* was decommissioned in 1947, a new nuclear-powered carrier with the same name joined the U.S. Navy in 1958.

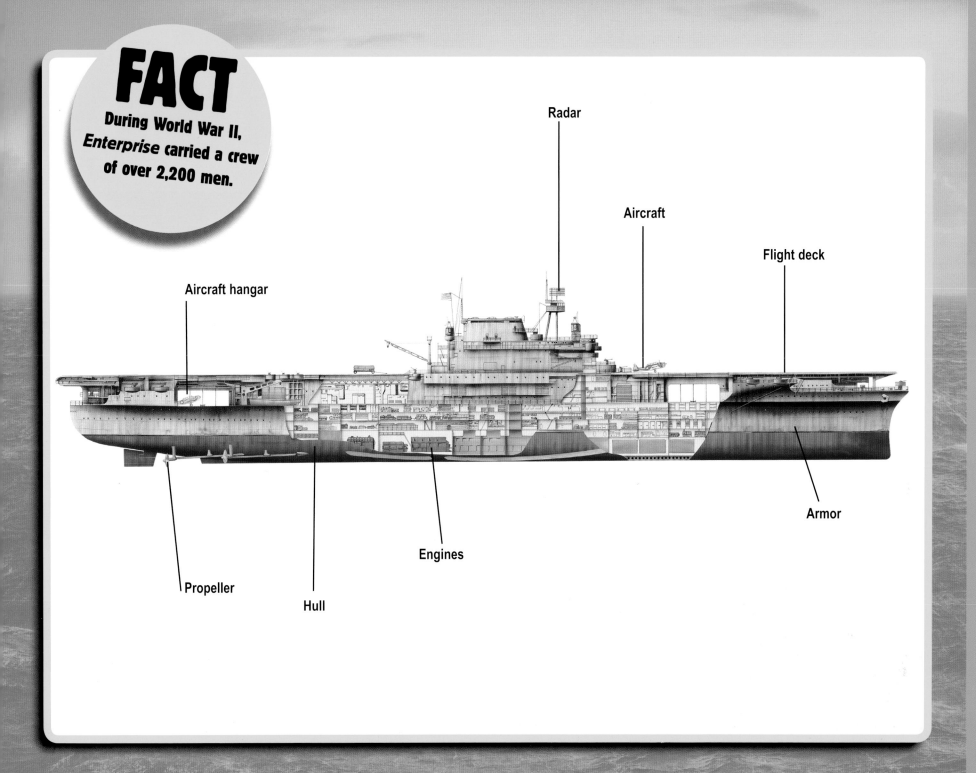

FACT
During World War II, *Enterprise* carried a crew of over 2,200 men.

Radar

Aircraft

Flight deck

Aircraft hangar

Armor

Engines

Propeller

Hull

KMS Bismarck (1939)

The German battleship *Bismarck* was named in honor of Otto von Bismarck, the first leader of a unified Germany. The main role of *Bismarck* was to raid U.S. and British shipping routes in the Atlantic Ocean.

Construction of *Bismarck* began in the summer of 1936. The ship was launched in the winter of 1939. *Bismarck* proved to be a giant among all the other battleships of the period, weighing in at 50,000 tons.

Super Battleship

Protected by thick armor and armed with massive guns, the Royal Navy feared that *Bismarck* would be a menace to Britain's merchant fleet in the Atlantic. At the time of

The namesake of the "Iron Chancellor," *Bismarck* was the pride and joy of the German navy.

In addition to her main guns, *Bismarck* was also armed with smaller cannons, machine guns, and antiaircraft weapons.

her completion, *Bismarck* weighed in at 100 million pounds (46 million kg). The ship was protected by strong armor measuring over 14 inches (360 mm) thick. The warship was built with eight 15-inch (380 mm) guns. Four turrets were built on deck, each holding two guns. Two turrets were placed **forward** and two **aft**. Along with the main guns, twelve smaller cannons were positioned on the sides of the ship.

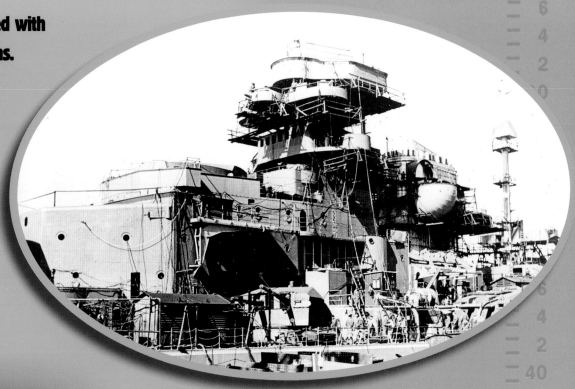

Did you know?

• *Bismarck* was sunk by torpedoes launched by airplanes and a cruiser.

• Only 110 men out of a crew of 2,200 survived the attack.

The Hunt for Bismarck

Bismarck was a huge threat to the British Royal Navy. She destroyed the British battle cruiser HMS *Hood* and damaged the battleship *Prince of Wales*. Though *Bismarck* proved to be a difficult target for the Allies, her luck changed on May 26, 1941. After being hunted down by British warships and torpedo bombers, *Bismarck* was sunk in the North Atlantic.

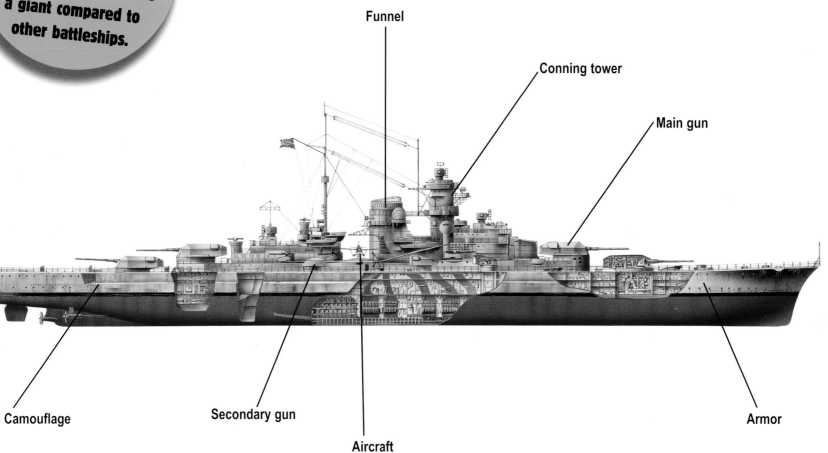

FACT
At over 800 feet long (250 m), *Bismarck* was a giant compared to other battleships.

Funnel

Conning tower

Main gun

Camouflage

Secondary gun

Aircraft

Armor

昭和15年9月20日　1号艦　8時44分

26

Yamato (1940)

Yamato was the largest battleship ever built. She served the Japanese Imperial Navy during World War II, fighting in the Pacific against the U.S. Navy. *Yamato's* size and weapons outmatched the American battleships.

• • • • • • • • • • • • • •

Construction of the battleship started in late 1940. The building of the ship was kept secret with few people knowing all the design details. By the time the ship was completed on December 16, 1941, *Yamato*—along with her sister ship *Musashi*—was the most powerful battleship ever sent to sea.

Supership Yamato

Weighing in at over 72,800 tons, the battleship *Yamato* was often referred to as a "supership." Armed with nine

Due to her size and weight, *Yamato* was slower than other battleships of that time.

Yamato's main guns could fire on targets as far as 25 miles (40 km) away!

attacked by American dive bomber planes based on U.S. aircraft carriers. Without a strong **defense** against an air attack, Yamato suffered a great deal of damage from bombs, torpedoes, and rockets. Yamato's crew was ordered to abandon ship, but it was too late. Out of a crew of around 2,800 men, only a few hundred were saved.

18-inch (460 mm) main guns and thick armor, Yamato was meant to be a symbol of Japan's power. At the time, many considered Yamato superior to battleships built by other countries.

Final Voyage

While on her way to the Japanese island of Okinawa, Yamato and the rest of the warships in her group were

Did you know?

• **World War II proved that the aircraft carrier was a more effective weapon than the battleship.**

• **The U.S. Navy lost ten airplanes during the attack that sank Yamato.**

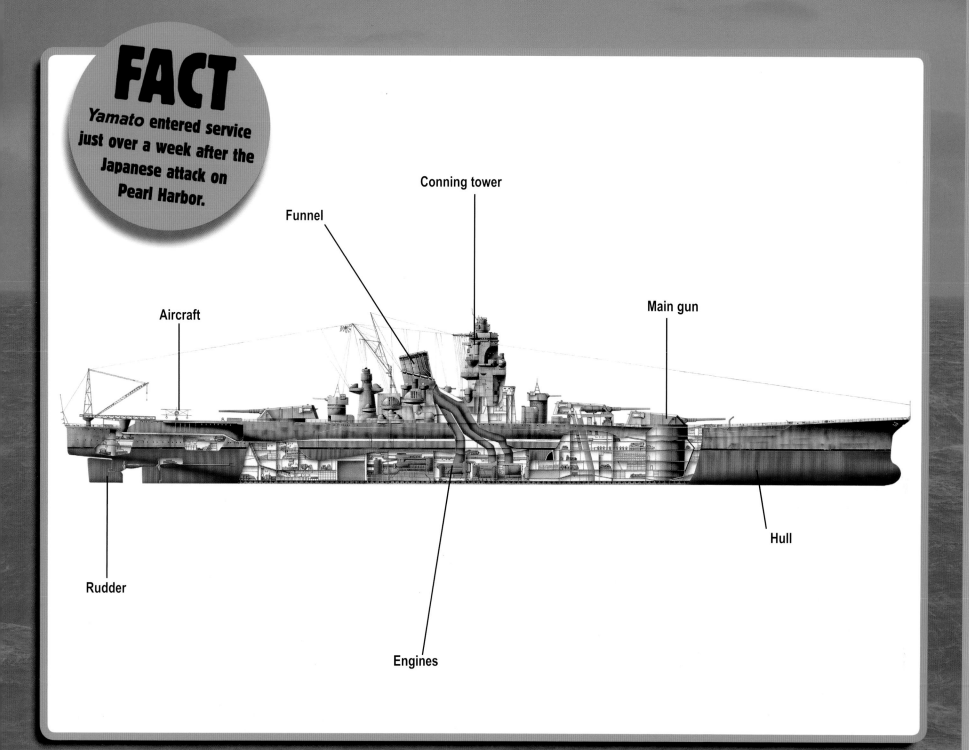

FACT
Yamato entered service just over a week after the Japanese attack on Pearl Harbor.

Conning tower

Funnel

Aircraft

Main gun

Rudder

Hull

Engines

USS Iowa (1942)

The U.S.-built *Iowa* was launched in 1942. She served in the U.S. Navy for close to 40 years, fighting during World War II and in the Korean War (1950–1953). She was one of the longest serving ships in the U.S. fleet.

The battleship *Iowa* was part of a new class of warships. She was built to be faster than the giant battleships built by the Japanese, but with enough **firepower** to go against any threat.

Tokyo Bay

USS *Iowa* faced the Japanese Imperial Navy in many key battles fought in the Pacific, including the Battle of the Philippine Sea and the Battle Leyte Gulf. With the defeat of Japan in 1945, USS *Iowa* joined the American

Narrower and lighter than many of the other battleships, *Iowa* was able to travel at higher speeds.

- During World War II, *Iowa's* crew numbered over 2,000 men.

- USS *Iowa* received 11 battle stars for her years of service in the U.S. Navy.

included Tomahawk cruise missiles, Harpoon anti-ship missiles, and other advanced weapons systems. This upgrade added to the battleship's firepower and defense capabilities.

Although refitted with the latest weapons and upgraded technologies during the 1980s, *Iowa's* original main guns still produced an impressive show of firepower.

forces sent to occupy Japan. She was made the **flagship** of the U.S. Fifth Fleet stationed in Tokyo Bay until 1949.

Modernization

Originally armed with nine 16-inch (400 mm) main cannons, and dozens of antiaircraft guns, USS *Iowa* went through a stage of modernization in 1982. New weapons added to the ship

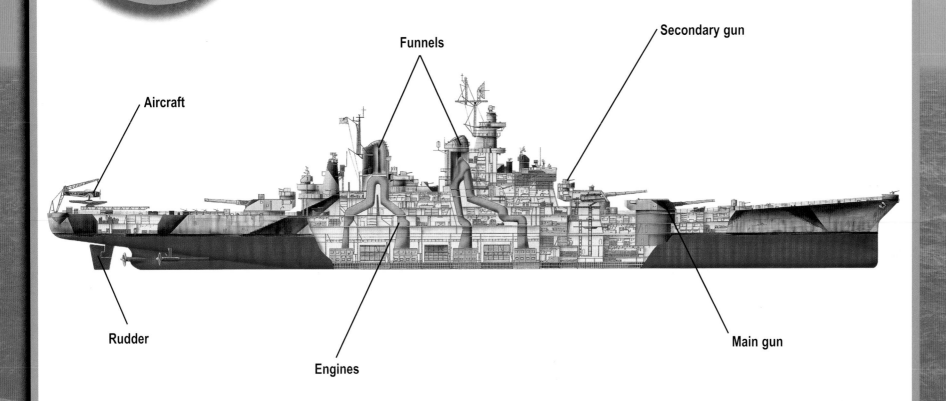

Funnels

Secondary gun

Aircraft

Rudder

Main gun

Engines

USS Nimitz (1972)

USS *Nimitz* is one of the largest warships in the world. Construction began in 1972. Put into service in 1975, this giant aircraft carrier is expected to stay in the U.S. Navy until the year 2030.

Aircraft carriers are a huge investment. They cost millions of dollars to run and operate. Not including its aircraft, the construction cost for USS *Nimitz* was close to $5 billion.

Nuclear Power

Nimitz is a nuclear-powered aircraft carrier. A **nuclear reactor** provides the ship with all of her power. Unlike earlier ships, which were fueled by coal, diesel,

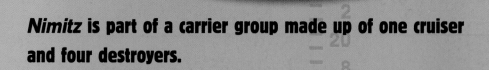

***Nimitz* is part of a carrier group made up of one cruiser and four destroyers.**

or gas, nuclear power allows *Nimitz* to operate for several years without ever needing to refuel. This provides the ship with the ability to stay out at sea as long as necessary.

The flight deck of *Nimitz* is over 1,000 feet (305 m) long.

Did you know?

• USS *Nimitz* was named after U.S. admiral Chester W. Nimitz (1885–1966).

• This "supercarrier" holds a crew of close to 6,000 people.

Attack Carrier

Aircraft carriers play a very important role. They protect other ships in the fleet and are also used to launch fighter jets against enemy targets at sea and on land. USS *Nimitz* carries 90 to 100 warplanes, including the latest fighter jets. She is also armed with a number of missile systems that can be used to destroy enemy ships and planes.

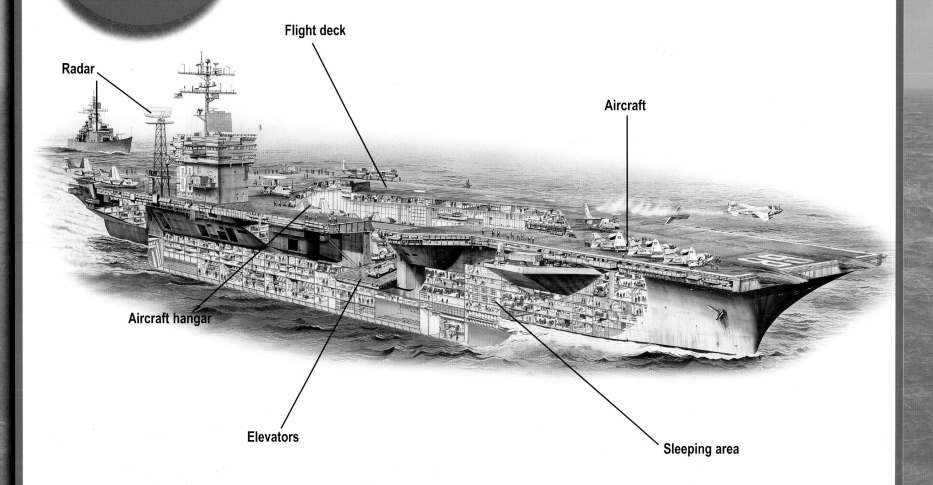

FACT

USS *Nimitz* is one of ten aircraft carriers currently serving in the U.S. Navy.

Flight deck

Radar

Aircraft

Aircraft hangar

Elevators

Sleeping area

USS Tarawa (1973)

Unlike the attack carrier *Nimitz*, which counts on her aircraft for attack and defense missions, USS *Tarawa* was built to serve as an amphibious assault ship.

Tarawa was used to transport and unload soldiers and equipment for land assaults. She was capable of carrying thousands of troops, heavy guns, and dozens of combat vehicles—including tanks.

Amphibious Assault Ship

Although she was not as large or as heavy as other aircraft carriers, *Tarawa*'s flight deck was able to

Tarawa carried six Harrier attack jets capable of vertical takeoff and landing, almost like a helicopter.

Amphibious assault ships can travel at a top speed of 25 knots—or 29 miles per hour (47 km/h).

and support to people in need. They are often sent to assist in delivering food, water, and support personnel—including doctors—to places that have experienced a natural disaster such as an earthquake or tsunami.

launch close to two dozen helicopters and **VTOL** aircraft. The helicopters helped support missions, land troops, and evacuate people in times of danger. Landing craft, including **hovercraft**, were released from the rear of the ship.

Humanitarian Support

In addition to serving a military role, amphibious assault ships also help provide supplies, equipment,

Did you know?

• Landing craft help transport equipment and troops to shore. USS *Tarawa's* crew included 2,000 Marines and close to 1,000 navy staff.

• After serving in the U.S. Navy for over 30 years, *Tarawa* was decommissioned in 2009.

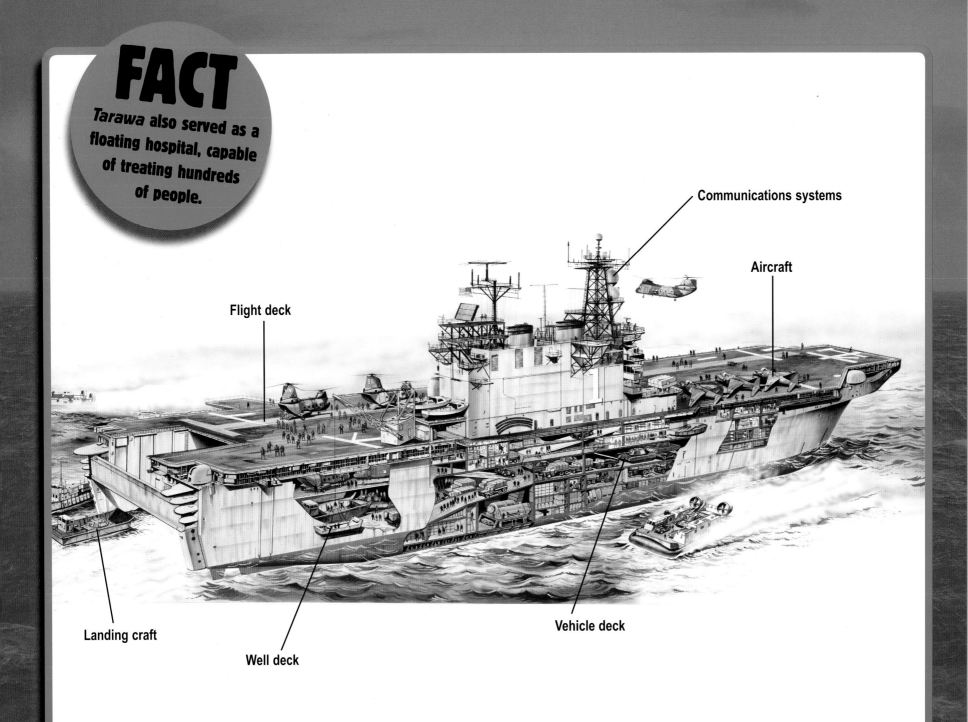

FACT
Tarawa also served as a floating hospital, capable of treating hundreds of people.

Communications systems

Aircraft

Flight deck

Landing craft

Well deck

Vehicle deck

HMS Invincible (1977)

HMS *Invincible* was a light British aircraft carrier. She began her service in the Royal Navy in the late 1970s and served in the Falklands War (1982) against Argentina, as well as in Operation Iraqi Freedom (2003).

Much like USS *Enterprise*, there were six other British navy ships named *Invincible*. The first one was built in the 1700s.

Aircraft

Invincible was able to carry up to 25 aircraft, including fighter jets and helicopters. Unlike other aircraft

Invincible's runway was 557 feet (170 m) long and included a ramp that sloped upward.

The carrier HMS *Invincible* operated as the command ship for all the warships in her group.

carriers, *Invincible*'s flight deck was shorter and narrower. A sloped ramp ran most of the ship's length. This ramp helped jets gain height during takeoff.

Did you know?

- *Invincible*'s **crew was made up of 1,000 personnel.**

- **After serving for close to 30 years, she was decommissioned in 2005.**

Countermeasures

Most navy warships include **countermeasures** to help defend against attack. *Invincible*'s countermeasures consisted of electronics that helped **jam** an enemy submarine's or ship's tracking abilities. They also included **decoys** that were able to confuse enemy torpedoes, missiles, or radar systems.

FACT
If *Invincible* was needed for service it would take 18 months to get her ready for war.

Radar

Aircraft

Helicopters

Missiles

Sleeping area

Engines

Flight deck

Glossary

aft—the back part of a ship

arms race—competition between countries to gather more and better weapons

battle cruiser—a naval ship built to be faster than a battleship

battle star—an award given to a military ship's crew for service during times of war

commission—officially enter a vessel into the navy

countermeasures—a defensive move used to "counter" (respond) to an attack

decommissioned—a ship that is officially removed from the navy

decoy—objects used to lead or attract enemy missiles or torpedoes away from their intended target

defense—protection against attack

dive bomber—a warplane designed specifically to drop bombs

firepower—the destructive force of guns, missiles, or other military weapons

flagship—the lead ship of a naval group that carries the commander

forward—the front part of a ship

hangar—location where aircraft are stored

horsepower—a unit of power

hovercraft—a vehicle for traveling over land or water that uses fans directed downward to create a cushion of air to hold it up

jam—to cause interference

knots—a unit of measurement used to show distance traveled at sea

launch—to set a completed ship into the water for the first time

merchant ship—a civilian ship used to carry cargo

nuclear reactor—the equipment where nuclear energy is used to produce power

propelled—to move forward

radar—an electronic device used to find the position of things

rearmament—rebuilding and regathering military weapons and equipment

turbine—an engine that operates by pressure of water, steam, or gas

turret—the rotating structure on a warship that holds the main guns

VTOL—a shortened term used for vertical takeoff and landing

Index

aircraft carriers 18–21, 28, 34–7, 42–5
amphibious assault ships 38–41
Arado Ar-196 sea plane 16
Argentina 43
armor 8
   Germany 17, 23, 24, 25
   Japan 28
   United Kingdom 12, 13
   United States 21
arms race 7, 8, 46

battle cruisers 10–13, 46
battle stars 32, 46
battleships 6–9, 14–17, 22–33
Bismarck, KMS 11, 12, 22–25

Ciliax, Captain Otto 15
countermeasures 44, 46

dive bombers 19, 28, 46
Doolittle Raid (1942) 19
Dreadnought, HMS 6–9
Duke of York, HMS 16

electronic countermeasures 44
English Channel 16
Enterprise, USS 18–21

Falklands War (1982) 43

France 8, 15

Germany 8, 11, 12, 14–17, 22–25
Gneisenau, KMS 15
Guadalcanal, Battle of (1942) 20
gun turrets 7, 8, 9, 15, 24, 25, 29, 32, 47

Harpoon anti-ship missiles 32
Harrier jets 39, 43
helicopters 39, 40, 43, 45
Hood, HMS 10–13, 24
hovercraft 40, 47
humanitarian support 40

Invincible, HMS 42–45
Iowa, USS 30–33
Iraq 43

Japan 8, 19, 20, 26–29, 31–32

Korean War (1950–1953) 31

Leyte Gulf, Battle of (1944) 20, 31

Musashi (Japan) 27

naming of ships 12, 33
Nimitz, Admiral Chester W. 36
Nimitz, USS 34–37, 39
nuclear power 35–36, 47

Okinawa 28
Operations
   Cerberus 15–16
   Iraqi Freedom 43

Pearl Harbor 19, 20, 29
Philippine Sea, Battle of the (1944) 20, 31
Prince of Wales, HMS 24

radar 44, 47
   United Kingdom 16, 45
   United States 21, 37

Scharnhorst, KMS 14–17
sea planes 16, 17

Tarawa, USS 38–41
Tomahawk cruise missiles 32
torpedoes 16, 19, 24, 28, 44
turbine engines 8, 47

United Kingdom 6–13, 16, 23–24, 42–45
United States 8, 18–21, 27, 28, 30–41

VTOL aircraft 39, 40, 43, 47

World War I 7, 8, 11
World War II 11, 12, 15–16, 19–20, 23–24,
   26–33, 31–32

Yamato (Japan) 26–29

forward—the front part of a ship

hangar—location where aircraft are stored

horsepower—a unit of power

hovercraft—a vehicle for traveling over land or water that uses fans directed downward to create a cushion of air to hold it up

jam—to cause interference

knots—a unit of measurement used to show distance traveled at sea

launch—to set a completed ship into the water for the first time

merchant ship—a civilian ship used to carry cargo

nuclear reactor—the equipment where nuclear energy is used to produce power

propelled—to move forward

radar—an electronic device used to find the position of things

rearmament—rebuilding and regathering military weapons and equipment

turbine—an engine that operates by pressure of water, steam, or gas

turret—the rotating structure on a warship that holds the main guns

VTOL—a shortened term used for vertical takeoff and landing

Index